GREAT AUSSIE SPORTS

ATHLETICS

DAVID RAFFERTY

REDBACK publishing

Redback Publishing
PO Box 357 Frenchs Forest NSW 2086
Australia

www.redbackpublishing.com.au
orders@redbackpublishing.com.au

978-1-925860-04-7 PBK

Author: David Rafferty
Editor: Caroline Thomas
Designer: Redback Publishing

Original illustrations © Redback Publishing 2022
Originated by Redback Publishing
Printed and bound in Malaysia

A catalogue record for this book is available from the National Library of Australia

Acknowledgements
Abbreviations: l—left, r—right, b—bottom, t—top, c—centre, m—middle
We would like to thank the following for permission to reproduce photographs: (Images © shutterstock) and (images@ Alamy Stock Photo)

p5t Sally Pearson, by Craig Franklin [CC BY-SA 3.0 au (https://creativecommons.org/licenses/by-sa/3.0/au/deed.en), via Wikimedia Commons,
p6t Central Park (Stawell Gift) Pano, Stawell, Vic, jjron, 12.01.201, by jjron [GFDL 1.2 (http://www.gnu.org/licenses/old-licenses/fdl-1.2.html)], via Wikimedia Commons,
p6tm Gold-gld25a (from Victoria, Australia), by Rob Lavinsky, iRocks.com – CC-BY-SA-3.0 [CC BY-SA 3.0 (https://creativecommons.org/licenses/by-sa/3.0)], via Wikimedia Commons,
p6b Betty Cuthbert, Marlene Mathews, Heather Armitage, 1956 Olympics, by Tidningarnas Telegrambyrå [Public domain], via Wikimedia Commons,
p7bl Herb Elliott 1960c, author unknown (Mondadori Publishers) [Public domain], via Wikimedia Commons,
p7br Anthony 'Nick' Winter Part of collection: Jeux Olympiques de 1924.; Official postcrd no. 424 [Public Domain], courtesy of the National Library of Australia,
p8 Tampere, Finland, July 13: Kristlin Gear from Usa and Montanna Mcavoy from Australia running 3000 metres steeplechase in the IAAF World U20 Championship in Tampere, Finland 13t July, 2018, by Denis Kuvaev, via Shutterstock,
p9t Cathy Freeman (cropped), by Jason Pini/AusAID [CC BY 2.0 (https://creativecommons.org/licenses/by/2.0)], via Wikimedia Commons,
p12t Shirley Strickland de la Hunty by Laurie Sullivan, courtesy of Steve Given, via Flickr.com, accessible: (https://www.flickr.com/photos/69559277@N04/15923377163)
p12m Melbourne, Australia- June 5, 2014: The statue of Elizabeth Betty Cuthbert, an Australian athlete at Melbourne Cricket Ground in Australia, courtesy of e X p o s e, via Shutterstock.com
p12b Herb Elliott 1960d, author unknown (Mondadori Publishers) [Public domain], via Wikimedia Commons,
p13t Betty Cuthbert, c. 1950s, by Ted Hood [Public domain], via Wikimedia Commons,
p13b Cathy Freeman 2000 olympics, by Ian @ ThePaperboy.com [CC BY-SA 2.0 (https://creativecommons.org/licenses/by-sa/2.0)], via Wikimedia Commons,
p14t Osaka07 D6A Jana Rawlinson celebrating, by Eckhard Pecher (Arcimboldo) [CC BY 2.5 (https://creativecommons.org/licenses/by/2.5)], via Wikimedia Commons,
p14m Patrick Johnson, courtesy of Patrick Johnson,
p14b 20080308 Tamsyn Lewis, by Erik van Leeuwen [GFDL (http://www.gnu.org/copyleft/fdl.html)], via Wikimedia Commons,
p19t Dani Samuels Doha 2015, by Doha Stadium Plus Qatar from Doha, Qatar [CC BY 2.0 (https://creativecommons.org/licenses/by/2.0)], via Wikimedia Commons,
p25m Donetsk, Ukraine - Feb.11: Opening Ceremony of the Samsung Pole Vault Stars meeting on February 11, 2012 in Donetsk, Ukraine. By Denis Kuvaev, via Shutterstock,
p26 Yokohama, Japan - Saturday May 11 2019: Catriona Bisset and Joshua Ralph of Australia after the mixed 2x2x400m relay during Day 1 of the 2019 IAAF World Relay Championships at the Nissan Stadium, by Roger Sedres, via Shutterstock,
p27 Yokohama, Japan - Saturday May 11 2019: Aleia Hobbs, Dezerea Bryant, Ashley Henderson and Mikiah Brisco of the USA 4x100m relay team during the 2019 IAAF World Relay Championships, by Roger Sedres, via Shutterstock,

CONTENTS

TRACK AND FIELD

Athletics involves a number of sports grouped into two areas: racing in track events and throwing or jumping in field events. Australia's elite track and field athletes represent the nation at top international competitions. At the 2000 Olympics, Cathy Freeman captured the attention and hearts of the nation when she won the gold medal for the 400 metres sprint. Field champions, Jai Taurima and Tatiana Grigorieva inspired millions with their achievements, winning Olympic silver medals in **long jump** and **pole vault** respectively.

At the 2018 Gold Coast Commonwealth Games, athletes such as Kathryn Mitchell, Brandon Starc, Kurtis Marschall and Dani Stevens won gold medals.

For Everyone

Athletics is walking, running, throwing and jumping. Running along a beach and walking the dog around the park are as much athletics activities as the long jump and 100 metres sprint. Without realising it, many people do athletics activities every day.

Athletics has a strong following in Australia at all levels. Children as young as five participate in **Little Athletics** in every state and territory. The official figure for participation by young people in athletics competitions is 100,000 at almost 500 centres across the country. Many more Australians over the age of 15 take part in athletics events, including club sports meets, fun runs, mini-marathons and **cross-country** runs. There are also millions of Australians who belong to jogging clubs and fitness clubs.

Athletics at the Olympics

Athletics competitions date back to the original Olympics, held in Greece in 776 **BCE**. At the first modern Olympic Games, held in Athens in 1896, Australia won two gold medals in athletics events and has competed at every Olympics since then. Australian athletes won three medals in the London 2012 campaign, with Sally Pearson breaking the Olympic record to win 100m hurdles gold. At the 2016 Rio Olympics, four-time Olympic medallist Jared Tallent won silver for the 50 kilometre walk, and Dane-Bird Smith won bronze for the 20 kilometre walk.

IN 2012, SALLY PEARSON BROKE THE OLYMPIC RECORD FOR THE 100M HURDLES

Olympic Athletics Events

Athletics events at the Olympics can be divided into four sections: track, field, road and combined. Track events include: sprints (100m, 200m, 400m), middle-distance running (800m and 1,500m), long-distance running (5km and 10km), hurdling (100m and 400m for women, 110m and 400m for men), relays (4 x 100m and 4 x 400m) and the men's three kilometre **steeplechase**. Field events, for both men and women, include the long jump, **triple jump**, **high jump**, pole vault, shot put, **discus**, **javelin** and hammer throw. Road events consist of the men's and women's **marathons**, the men's 20 kilometre and 50 kilometre race walks and the women's 20 kilometre race walk. Combined events include the **heptathlon** for women and the **decathlon** for men.

HISTORY OF ATHLETICS IN AUSTRALIA

Australian athletics began with the sporting games of some Aboriginal groups before European settlement. These athletics competitions, like those of the ancient Greeks at the first Olympics, were based on the skills of hunting and fighting. Spear-throwing contests were the forerunners of javelin throwing. Running, jumping and hurdling contests displayed the skills used in hunting prey.

CENTRAL PARK IN STAWELL, VICTORIA, IS HOME TO AUSTRALIA'S OLDEST AND RICHEST FOOT RACE, THE STAWELL GIFT.

Glory Years

Over the years, numerous athletics heroes have captured the attention of the nation. Australian Olympians such as Edwin Flack, Nick Winter and John Winter were hailed as heroes. In the years following World War II (1939-1945), Australian athletics entered a golden age. Marjorie Jackson, Shirley Strickland de la Hunty, Betty Cuthbert, Herb Elliott and Ralph Doubell were world champions. In terms of population, Australia was the most successful athletics nation in the world. In the 1980s, athletes such as Glynis Nunn and Debbie Flintoff-King kept the flag flying. At the turn of the century, a host of new athletes including Cathy Freeman, Jana Pittman, Patrick Johnson and Tatiana Grigorieva, bursting with talent and dedication, made Australia a formidable force in world athletics once again.

European Settlers

European settlers began competing with each other in athletics as early as 1800. In the 1850s and 1860s, professional foot races with valuable prizes of gold nuggets began on the goldfields of Victoria and Western Australia. The famous Stawell Gift foot race dates from this time. By the early 1900s, state and national athletics associations had been set up to organise the competitions.

BETTY CUTHBERT WINS 1956 WOMEN'S 100 METRES FINAL,

Amateur Athletics Gets Started

The first **amateur** athletics club was formed in Adelaide in 1867. That same year, New South Wales formed the first colony-wide athletics association to organise and govern competitions as more new clubs quickly formed throughout the colonies. Amateur athletes, unlike the professionals, did not accept money for participating, and all athletes were male. It was many years before female athletes were recognised.

Drugs in Athletics

Over recent decades, some unethical athletes have used illegal performance-enhancing drugs. When this happens, supporters can feel very sad and confused by the betrayal of trust, and the many other honest athletes can feel cheated and angry.

Sadly, many instances of illegal drug use have been uncovered, despite very strict laws that exist to control drug use in athletics. During the course of each year, thousands of athletes all over the world are screened for drug use and penalties can include a lifetime competition ban.

Athletics Australia administers a program of drug testing in Australia, and the International Association of Athletic Federations (IAAF) carries out a program of testing international athletes.

Early Records

Records show that races were being held in Sydney's Hyde Park in 1810. A local by the name of Dicky Dowling went into the record books as the first European sprint champion, regularly winning races over 50 yards (about 47 metres).

NICK WINTER WAS THE FIRST AUSTRALIAN TO WIN AN OLYMPIC GOLD MEDAL IN A FIELD EVENT. HE WON GOLD IN THE TRIPLE JUMP AT THE 1924 OLYMPIC GAMES.

Athletics in the Modern Era

By 1910, every state of the new nation of Australia had an amateur athletics association. The **Australian Track and Field Championships (ATFC)**, first staged in 1890, saw athletes from both the Australian and New Zealand colonies competing against each other. In 1929, women were permitted to enter the ATFC for the first time. By the 1950s, Australian track athletes such as Marjorie Jackson, Shirley Strickland and Betty Cuthbert dominated sprinting events, and in the 1960s Herb Elliott and Ron Clarke set middle distance records.

HERB ELLIOTT AT THE 1960 OLYMPICS

THE TRACK – RUNNING

There are 14 major track events for men and women, ranging from sprints, which can take as little as 10 seconds, to the gruelling marathon, which takes over two hours.

Sprint Events

The main sprint events are the 100, 200 and 400 metres. When events are run outdoors, **wind assistance** is taken into account.

Sprinters must stay within their designated lane. No competitor may commence racing until the starting pistol is fired. Any competitor who spoils a start by moving his or her shoulders at the 'get set' signal is given a warning. If the competitor again spoils the start, he or she is **disqualified**.

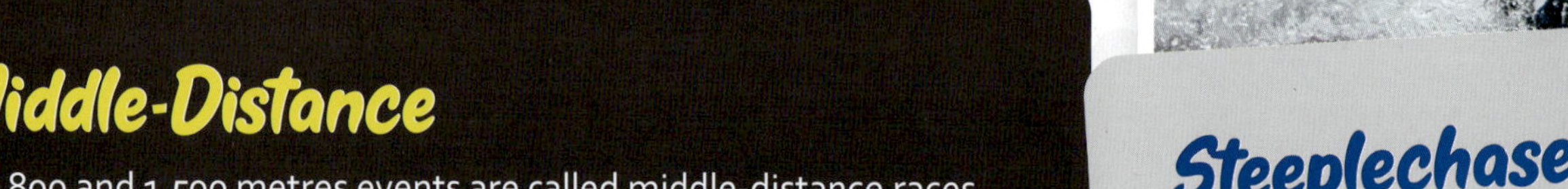

Middle-Distance

The 800 and 1,500 metres events are called middle-distance races to distinguish them from the sprints and long-distance events. Both events are run on indoor and outdoor tracks, with wind assistance taken into account for outdoor runs.

In the 800 metres, runners must stay within their designated lanes for the first two bends. They may then change lanes, but only without deliberately interfering with any other runner. In the 1,500 metres, runners can change lanes at any time, but only without impeding others. Any runner who carelessly or deliberately gets in the way of another runner may be disqualified.

Steeplechase

The steeplechase is run over 3,000 metres. Competitors jump 28 fixed obstacles, such as fences and hurdles, and clear seven water jumps. Steeplechasers may stand on or jump over the obstacles while racing. Chasers may not deliberately interfere with another competitor.

Long-Distance Events

The 5,000, 6,000 and 10,000 metres long distance runs are held on indoor and outdoor tracks. Wind assistance is not taken into account. Each circuit of the track is 400 metres, so a 5,000 metre runner completes 12.5 circuits, a 6,000 metre runner completes 15 circuits, and a 10,000 metre runner completes 25 circuits.

Runners may change lanes at any time, as long as they do not interfere with other runners. Deliberate or careless obstruction of another runner may lead to disqualification.

Marathon

The Olympic marathon is run over a distance of 42.195 kilometres. It is always run outdoors and wind assistance is not considered. Runners are not permitted to deliberately interfere with other runners. There are many other competitive marathon events around Australia with competitors ranging from professional athletes to keen senior citizens.

CHAMPION PROFILE

CATHY FREEMAN

BORN: 16 FEBRUARY 1973
PLACE OF BIRTH: MACKAY, QLD
EVENTS: 100, 200, 400 METRES, 4 X 400 METRES RELAY

CAREER HIGHLIGHTS

- **4 X 100 GOLD MEDALLIST:** 1990 COMMONWEALTH GAMES
- **200 AND 400 METRES GOLD MEDALLIST:** 1994 COMMONWEALTH GAMES
- **400 METRES SILVER MEDALLIST:** 1996 OLYMPICS
- **400 METRES GOLD MEDALLIST:** 2000 OLYMPICS
- **4 X 400 RELAY GOLD MEDALLIST:** 2002 COMMONWEALTH GAMES
- **RETIRED FROM ATHLETICS IN 2003.**

AUSTRALIA'S GREATEST

LONG-DISTANCE RUNNER
WORLD RECORD
5,000 AND 10,000 METRES:
(1960S) RON CLARKE

MIDDLE-DISTANCE RUNNER
OLYMPIC GOLD
1,500 METRES:
(1960) HERB ELLIOTT

SPRINTER
OLYMPIC GOLD
400 METRES:
(1964) BETTY CUTHBERT
100, 200 AND 4 X 100 METRES:
(1956) BETTY CUTHBERT

MARATHON RUNNER
WINNER OF TWO MAJOR INTERNATIONAL MARATHONS:
(1980S) ROBERT DE CASTELLA

What is Wind Assistance?

If a competitor in a sprint race is helped by a tail wind, which is a wind blowing against the sprinter's back, wind assistance will be noted in the time recorded. If the wind assistance is greater than 1.2 metres over the distance of the race, the time cannot stand as a record. Wind assistance is measured electronically.

THE TRACK – RELAYS, HURDLES AND WALKING

Relays

The three principal **relay** events (4 x 100 metres, 4 x 200 metres and 4 x 400 metres) are all sprints. In relays, the lead sprinter starts the race, sprints the first leg, then while running passes a baton 30 centimetres long to the second sprinter. The second sprinter runs the second leg and passes the **baton** to the third sprinter, who runs the third leg and passes the baton to the final leg sprinter, who finishes the race. Smooth and quick baton changes are crucial in relay races.

Relay Rules

In the 4 x 100 metres and 4 x 200 metres relays, each sprinter must stay in the team's designated lane for the entire race. In the 4 x 400 metres relay, only the sprinter who runs the final leg may change lanes, usually to the inside lane. The baton must be carried for the entire race in all relays. If the baton is dropped, it must be picked up. If a runner crosses the finish line without the baton in his or her hand, the team is disqualified.

Hurdles

The women's hurdles events are run over a distance of 100 metres and 400 metres. The men's hurdles events are run over 110 metres and 400 metres. Each hurdler jumps 10 hurdles in the course of the race. The hurdles are 83.8 centimetres high for the women's 100m hurdles and 76.2 centimetres for the 400 metres hurdles. Men's hurdles are 106.7 centimetres high for the 110 metres hurdles, and 91.4 centimetres high for the 400 metres hurdles.

Hurdle Rules

Each hurdler must stay in his or her lane for the entire race. The hurdler must attempt to clear each hurdle, and must not deliberately knock a hurdle over. In the course of a race, hurdlers often knock over hurdles - they are not disqualified as long as the hurdles were knocked accidentally.

DURING THE COURSE OF A HURDLES EVENT, EACH HURDLER CLEARS 10 HURDLES.

Who Won?

In modern athletics, timing is electronic, from start to finish. Margins are recorded to within 0.001 of a second. In the 100 metres, winning by 0.001 of a second means winning by as little as half a millimetre.

AUSTRALIA'S GREATEST

WALKER

SET 30 WORLD RECORDS:
(1980S AND 1990S)
KERRY SAXBY-JUNNA

RELAY SPRINTERS

OLYMPIC GOLD
4 X 100M RELAY: (1956)
NORMA CROKER,
BETTY CUTHBERT,
FLEUR MELLOR
SHIRLEY STRICKLAND DE LA HUNTY

HURDLERS

THREE GOLD, ONE SILVER AND THREE OLYMPIC BRONZE:
SHIRLEY STRICKLAND DE LA HUNTY
OLYMPIC GOLD:
(1988) DEBBIE FLINTOFF-KING

Walking Races and Rules

The major walking events are conducted over distances from 20 to 100 kilometres. Most walking events are held outdoors. Participants attempt to walk as fast as possible without breaking into a run. At the Olympics, walking races are competed over 20 and 50 kilometres. Walkers must not allow both feet to entirely leave the ground at the same time. Competition walking looks very different to ordinary walking. When race walking, no visible (to the judges' eyes) loss of contact with the ground can take place. If a walker does not have at least a part of one foot on the ground for the entire race, he or she will be disqualified.

AUSTRALIA'S GREATS OF THE TRACK

SHIRLEY STRICKLAND DE LA HUNTY

Australia's greatest hurdler, Shirley Strickland de la Hunty, competed at three Olympics - London, in 1948, Helsinki,in 1952, and Melbourne, in 1956. In these Olympics she won three gold, one silver and two bronze medals, setting and breaking world records in the 80 metres hurdles. Her gold medals came at Helsinki (80 metres hurdles) and Melbourne (80 metres hurdles and 4 x 100 metres relay). Shirley set five world records during her career, including a world record for an event that was not her favourite, the 100 metres sprint.

BETTY CUTHBERT

Winner of four Olympic gold medals, Betty Cuthbert is considered the best track athlete ever to compete for Australia. Betty struggled with form early in 1956, but found her rhythm in time to record a world record for the 200 metres at trials for the Olympics. She competed in Melbourne in the 1956 Games with few people having heard of her. After the Olympics, she became famous worldwide. Betty won the 100 metres and the 200 metres, then ran an astonishing leg in the 4 x 100 metres relay to lead the Aussie team to victory. Injury ruined her chances of competing in the 1960 Rome Olympics, but she came back in 1964 to win her fourth gold medal in the 400 metres.

HERB ELLIOTT

Under the guidance of legendary coach Percy Cerutty, Herb Elliott was trained on the sand dunes of Portsea on Victoria's coast. Herb developed such extraordinary stamina that he was spoken of as 'the fittest man on Earth' when he went to Rome to represent Australia in the 1,500 metres. Already the world record holder in the event with a time of three minutes and 36 seconds, Herb went one better in the 1,500 metres final, winning in the new world record time of three minutes and 35 seconds.

The Right Friend at the Right Time

Betty Cuthbert was born in Merrylands, not far from Sydney. While participating in school sport at high school, she was lucky to have a former star athlete, Jane Ferguson, as her teacher. Ferguson recognised Cuthbert's ability and set her on the road to success, guiding and coaching her all the way. Betty was a shy girl, and without the strength and encouragement of her coach and friend, she may never have scaled the heights of greatness.

CATHY FREEMAN

Cathy Freeman is not only the most famous sportsperson in Australia, but one of our most admired athletes ever. At the 1990 Commonwealth Games, Cathy showed her talent in the 4 x 100 metres relay team, winning gold along with team members Monique Dunstan, Kathy Sambell and Kerry Johnson. More Commonwealth Games gold medals followed in 1994 with victories in the 200 and 400 metres sprints. Cathy became world champion in the 400 metres in 1997 and pushed herself to the limit to take the gold medal for the 400 metres at the Sydney 2000 Olympics. Cathy retired from athletics in 2003 but travelled to Athens in 2004 to support the athletics team.

JANA PITTMAN

Jana began her athletics career in 1996 at the age of 13. By age 15, Pittman had started to stamp herself as one of the future stars of Australian track and field. At the 2002 Commonwealth Games, Jana ran in the Australian relay team that won gold. At the 2003 World Athletics Championships, Jana won an unexpected gold medal in the 400 metres hurdles, then won gold again for the same event in the 2007 Olympics. At the 2006 Commonwealth Games she won another two gold medals. Pittman is one of only nine athletes to win world championships at the youth, junior, and senior level of an athletic event, and after taking up the two-woman bobsleigh, she was the first Australian female athlete to compete in both the Summer and Winter Olympic games.

PATRICK JOHNSON

Patrick Johnson is the current Australian record holder for the 100 metres sprint, with a time of 9.93 seconds. Being of Aboriginal and Irish descent, Johnson became the first person of non-African descent to break the 10-second barrier and is now the 17th fastest man in history and the 38th man to crack the 10 second barrier. In 2000, Johnson represented Australia at the Olympic Games and finished his career with a bronze medal in the 4 × 100 metres relay in the 2002 Commonwealth Games.

TAMSYN LEWIS

At the 1994 Commonwealth Games, 16 year old Tamsyn Lewis enjoyed her first taste of international competition. Already that year she had set a high standard for herself by making the finals of the 400 metres at the World Junior Championships. As the nation's leading female 800 metres runner, Tamsyn qualified for the 800 metres at the Sydney 2000 Olympics. She also ran a great leg of the 4 x 400 metres relay with Cathy Freeman. Tamsyn has won gold medals at each of the 1998, 2002 and 2006 Commonwealth Games, running in the 4 x 400 metres relay. She won a total of 18 Australian Championships at 400 metres, 800 metres and 400m hurdles.

AUSTRALIAN RECORDS AND RECORD HOLDERS

MEN		WOMEN
Patrick Johnson, 9.93	100m	Melissa Breen, 11.11
Peter Norman, 20.06	200m	Melinda Gainsford-Taylor, 22.23
Darren Clarke, 44.38	400m	Cathy Freeman, 48.63
Joseph Deng, 1:44.21	800m	Catriona Bisset, 1:58.78
Ryan Gregson, 3:31.06	1500m	Linden Hall, 4:00.86
Craig Mottram, 12:55.76	5000m	Benita Johnson-Willis, 14:47.60
Ben St Lawrence, 27:24.95	10,000m	Benita Johnson-Willis, 30:37.68
Kyle Vander-Kuyp, 13.29 (110m)	100-110m hurdles	Sally Pearson 12.28 (100m)
Rohan Robinson, 48.28	400m hurdles	Debbie Flintoff-King, 53.17
Nathan Deakes, 1:17:33	20km walk	Jane Saville, 1:27:44
Nathan Deakes, 3:35:47	50km walk	Claire Tallent, 4:09:33

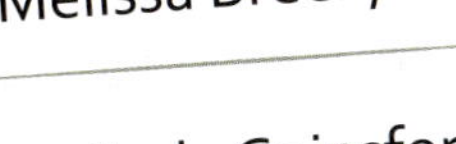

Time keeping

There is a standard way to show athletes' times:
30:23.42 =
30 minutes, 23. 42 seconds.

THE FIELD – JAVELIN AND SHOT PUT

Field events are divided into throwing, jumping and combined events. Throwing events include javelin, shot put, discus and hammer. Jumping events include high jump, pole vault, long jump and triple jump. Combined events include the decathlon for men and the heptathlon for women.

Javelin

The javelin is a modern version of the spear. It can have a wood, metal or fiberglass stick, but the point is always metal. The javelin must be between 260 and 270 centimetres in length for men, and between 220 and 230 centimetres for women. The minimum weight of the javelin is 800 grams for men, and 600 grams for women. The aim of the event is to throw the javelin as far as possible.

Javelin Rules

The javelin must be thrown from within an area marked with an arc on the ground, and must land within two lines that spread out from the top of the arc. The javelin must not touch the thrower's body or the ground while the athlete prepares to throw. The javelin must land tip first, but it does not have to stick in the ground. The length of the throw is judged from the throwing arc to the place where the tip of the javelin first touches the ground. If the throw is legal, the judges show a white flag, and the throw is measured. If the throw is illegal, the judges show a red flag. In most competitions, each competitor has three throws, with the top eight competitors allowed a further three throws. The competitor who is judged to have thrown the javelin the furthest wins.

THE DECATHLON

10 SECTIONS, USUALLY RUN OVER TWO DAYS. COMPETITORS GAIN POINTS IN EACH SECTION. THE WINNER HAS THE MOST POINTS AT THE END OF THE 10TH AND FINAL SECTION.

THE MEN'S DECATHLON CONSISTS OF:

DAY ONE:
100M SPRINT, LONG JUMP, SHOT PUT, HIGH JUMP, AND 400M

DAY TWO:
110M HURDLES, DISCUS THROW, POLE VAULT, JAVELIN THROW, AND 1500M RUN

THE WOMEN'S DECATHLON CONSISTS OF:

DAY ONE:
100M, DISCUS THROW, POLE VAULT, JAVELIN THROW, AND 400M

DAY TWO:
100M HURDLES, LONG JUMP, SHOT PUT, HIGH JUMP, AND 1500M RUN

THE RULES FOR EACH DECATHLON EVENT ARE THE SAME AS FOR THE INDIVIDUAL TRACK AND FIELD EVENTS.

IF A COMPETITOR MISSES ANY SECTION, THEY ARE CONSIDERED TO HAVE WITHDRAWN FROM THE COMPETITION.

Shot Put

In shot put, a competitor throws a round metal ball, or 'shot', as far as he or she can. For the men's competition, the shot weighs a minimum of 7.257 kilograms; for women, the minimum weight is four kilograms.

Shot Put Rules

The throw must be made from within a circle and must land within two marked side boundaries. The thrower cannot touch any part of the throwing circle line, including the **stopboard** at the front of the circle, and must use only one hand for the throw. The throw is measured from the front of the throwing circle to the point at which the shot first touches the ground. The judges show a white flag for a legal throw and a red flag for an illegal throw. In most competitions, each shot putter has three throws, with the top eight competitors allowed a further three throws. The competitor who has thrown the shot the furthest wins.

THE FIELD – DISCUS, HAMMER AND HIGH JUMP

Discus

The discus is a smooth metal plate, thicker at the centre than at the rim. For the men's event, the discus is 21.9 centimetres in diameter and weighs two kilograms; for the women's event, the discus is 18 centimetres in diameter and weighs one kilogram. The aim of the event is to throw the discus as far as possible from within a marked circle so that it lands within two marked side boundaries. Discus throwers use a turning technique to gain maximum force for the throw. The discus, when released, spins through the air.

Discus Rules

The throw must be completed within the throwing circle. The competitor must not touch any part of the circle's border with any part of his or her body during the throw or while the discus is in the air. Measurement for the throw is made from the top of the throwing circle to the first point at which the discus touches the ground. Judges show a white flag for a legal throw and a red flag for an illegal throw. Competitors are allowed three throws in the finals.

Hammer

The hammer is a metal ball attached to a length of metal cable with a handle. The men's hammer weighs 7.257 kilograms and is 121.3 centimetres long. The women's hammer is slightly shorter and weighs slightly less. The competitor throws the hammer from within a circle so that it lands within two marked side boundaries. Throwers use a spinning technique to gain maximum force for a throw.

Hammer Rules

The competitor must not touch the marked boundary of the throwing circle during the throw or while the hammer is in the air. The throw is measured from the top of the circle to the first point at which the hammer strikes the ground. The judges show a white flag for a legal throw and a red flag for an illegal throw. Competitors are allowed three throws in the finals.

CHAMPION PROFILE

DANI STEVENS
BORN: 26 MAY 1988
PLACE OF BIRTH: FAIRFIELD, NSW
EVENTS: DISCUS THROW

CAREER HIGHLIGHTS

- COMMONWEALTH GAMES GOLD: 2018

High Jump

Competitors attempt to jump over a bar held by two upright posts. The bar is raised higher after each group of jumpers have attempted to clear the bar. The competitor who completes the highest jump is the winner.

High Jump Rules

Each competitor is allowed three attempts at each jump. The competitor must take off for the jump from one foot. Competitors usually arch backwards to clear the bar. For a jump to be legal, the bar must stay in position even after the competitor has landed on the soft landing mat.

The Heptathlon

The heptathlon is made up of seven events, with competitors gaining points in each section. The winner is the competitor who has the greatest number of points at the end of the seventh and final section.

The men's heptathlon consists of:
Day one – 60m sprint, long jump, shot put and high jump
Day two – 60m hurdles, pole vault and 1000m run.

The women's heptathlon consists of:
Day one – 100m hurdles, high jump, shot put, 200m sprint
Day two – long jump, javelin throw, 800m run.

The rules for each heptathlon event are the same as for the individual track and field events. If a competitor misses any section, they are considered to have withdrawn from the competition.

THE FIELD – POLE VAULT, LONG JUMP AND TRIPLE JUMP

AUSTRALIA'S GREATEST

TRIPLE JUMPER
OLYMPIC GOLD: (1924) NICK WINTER.

LONG JUMPERS
OLYMPIC SILVER: (2012) MITCHELL WATT
(2000) JAI TAURIMA
(1984) GARY HONEY
(1948) BILL BRUCE

HIGH JUMPERS
OLYMPIC GOLD: (1948) JOHN WINTER
OLYMPIC SILVER: (1956) CHILLA PORTER
(1964) MICHELLE BROWN
OLYMPIC BRONZE: (1992) TIM FORSYTH

JAVELIN THROWER
OLYMPIC SILVER: (1996) LOUISE MCPAUL CURREY

HAMMER THROWER
OLYMPIC 5TH PLACE: (2000) DEBBIE SOSIMENKO

POLE VAULTERS
12 WORLD RECORDS: (1990S) EMMA GEORGE

DECATHLETE
OLYMPIC SILVER: (2000) TATIANA GRIGORIEVA
OLYMPIC 4TH PLACE: (1948) PETER MULLINS

HEPTATHLETE
OLYMPIC GOLD: (1984) GLYNIS NUNN

Triple Jump

The aim of the triple jump is to travel the furthest distance possible using a hop, step and long jump. In the first action (the hop), the competitor must land on the foot from which he or she took off. In the step action, the competitor must land on the opposite foot from the landing foot in the hop action. In the jump action, the competitor must take off before the take-off marker. Measurement is made from the start of the hop to the point at which the competitor's body first touches the sand in the jump section.

Pole Vault Rules

Each competitor can continue jumping until he or she records three consecutive failures to clear the bar. For a vault to be legal, the bar must remain in position even after the vaulter has landed on the mat. If the pole knocks the bar off, even after the vaulter has cleared the bar, the vault counts as a failure.

Pole Vault

Competitors attempt to clear a bar held between two upright posts using a long, flexible 'pole'. The competitor runs towards the bar with the pole held forwards, sinks the base of the pole into a shallow pit in the ground and swings up on the pole, bending it backwards. The pole vaulter clears the bar feet-first, and lands on a soft mat. The pole used may be of any length or thickness, as long as it is approved by the judges.

Long Jump Rules

Jumps are measured from the take-off line to the point at which any part of the competitor's body first touches the sand. In most competitions, jumpers each make three attempts, with the top eight competitors allowed a further three attempts. The jumper's run-up may be any length but the jumper must take off before the take-off board. If the jumper's foot touches the take-off board, the jump is illegal.

Long Jump

The aim of the event is to jump as far as possible. Competitors make a running start, then leap from just before a take-off marker, landing on a bed of sand.

COMMONWEALTH GAMES 2018

In April 2018, Australia hosted the Commonwealth Games on Queensland's Gold Coast. A team of 109 athletes represented Australia at the Commonwealth Games.

The Australian Athletics team won an extraordinary 13 gold, 13 silver and 10 bronze for a total of 36 medals, while Kurt Fearnley, Kathryn Mitchell, Henry Frayne and Dani Stevens all broke records.

GOLD MEDALS

20km walk	Dane Bird-Smith
F38 Shot Put	Cam Crombie
T54 Marathon	Madison de Rozario
T54 1500m	Madison de Rozario
T54 Marathon	Kurt Fearnley
T35 100m	Isis Holt
Pole Vault	Kurtis Marschall
Javelin Throw	Kathryn Mitchell)
20km Walk	Jemima Montag
T38 100m	Evan O'Hanlon
Marathon	Michael Shelley
High Jump	Brandon Starc
Discus Throw	Dani Stevens

SILVER MEDALS

T54 Marathon	Eliza Ault-Connell
T54 1500m	Angela Ballard
T38 100m	Rhiannon Clarke
T38 Long Jump	Erin Cleaver
Hammer Throw	Matthew Denny
T54 1500m	Kurt Fearnley
Long Jump	Henry Frayne
Hammer Throw	Alexandra Hulley
F38 Shot Put	Marty Jackson
Javelin Throw	Hamish Peacock
Javelin Throw	Kelsey-Lee Roberts
Long Jump	Brooke Stratton
Marathon	Lisa Weightman

BRONZE MEDALS

T35 100m	Brianna Coop
T38 Long Jump	Taylor Doyle
Decathlon	Cedric Dubler
110m Hurdles	Nic Hough
Pole Vault	Nina Kennedy
T54 1500m	Jake Lappin
800m	Luke Mathews
High Jump	Nicola McDermott
Hammer Throw	Lara Nielson
Marathon	Jessica Trengove

Great Sportsmanship

The world watched Australian trio Eloise Wellings, Madeline Hills and Celia Sullohern run in the 10,000m and then wait for and greet the final runner, Lineo Chaka of Lesotho, who came in last place over five minutes behind the winner. Their act of support went viral around the internet.

THE ROLE OF MEDIA

Australians take sporting heroes to their hearts, encouraged by newspapers, radio, magazines and television. As early as the first Olympic Games of the modern era, held in Athens in 1896, newspapers helped fuel the interest of Australians in athletics heroes. One hundred and four years and 23 Olympics later, the largest audience in Australian television history watched Cathy Freeman take the gold medal for the 400 metres at the 2000 Sydney Olympics.

The Internet

Many people now watch sport online using their computer or personal device. They can livestream an event or watch it later.

The Power of Television

Sporting events are rated amongst the top four forms of television entertainment. Sponsors are prepared to pay large sums of money to promote products and services when athletics are shown on television, especially at major events such as the Olympic Games. The top athletes are professional sportspeople, and they are paid large sums of money. But it all begins with success on the sporting field.

How Sponsorship Works

Sponsorship is the practice of businesses paying individual athletes to promote their products and services. Top athletes sometimes sign contracts worth millions of dollars that require them to endorse one company alone. An athlete may have a number of contracts in different fields: one for sporting gear, one for a mobile phone company and one for a food manufacturer.

Sponsors also pay a lot of money to athletics organisations, such as Athletics Australia, in order to be associated with the success of that organisation. The national athletics championships, for example, carry the name of their sponsor. The money from sponsorship of this sort helps to support athletics as a whole sport, not just the **elite** athletes themselves.

Anywhere in the World

Free-to-air and pay television stations have a huge appetite for sport. Every major athletics event in the world is shown on television, from Grand Prix events to the World Athletics Championships and national athletics championships.

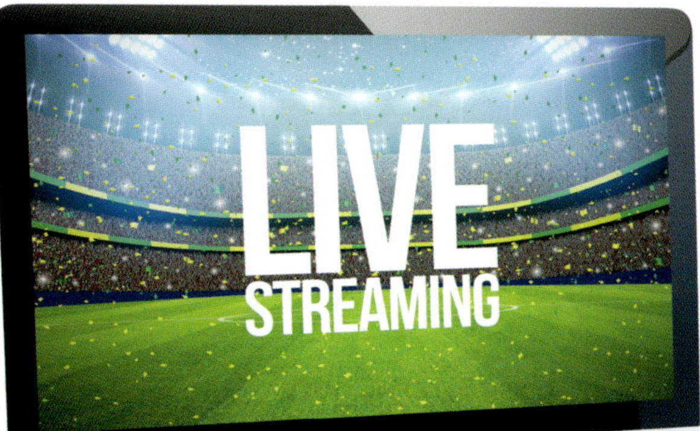

Did you Know?

After Edwin Flack's triumph in Athens, in 1896, he returned to Australia and continued in his occupation as an accountant. He made no money out of athletics and was rarely spoken of after his return.

Sport and Entertainment

The opening and closing ceremonies of the Sydney Olympics in 2000 attracted large television audiences. Australia broke viewing records with the whole Olympic event attracting over 36 billion viewing hours globally and an average of 46 hours per Australian viewer!

MAJOR NATIONAL AND INTERNATIONAL CHAMPIONSHIPS

Track and field are year-round careers for elite athletes, with competitions over the entire globe. The two biggest seasons for Australian athletes are the southern hemisphere summer, when they compete locally, and the northern hemisphere summer, when they compete in Europe and North America.

Serious local competition begins with the state titles, when athletes compete in the championships of their individual states. Athletes who meet qualifying times are eligible for participation in the Australian Athletics Championships. At these championships, athletes compete in various age groups, such as open, under 20, under 18, under 16 and under 14.

World Athletics Championships

The second most important competition in international athletics is the World Athletics Championships. These championships are held every second year, and only athletes who meet very high selection criteria are eligible to participate.

International Competition

Most of the major international competitions are organised through the International Association of Athletic Federations (IAAF). The most important of the IAAF competitions is the Diamond League.

Olympic and Commonwealth Games

Taking part in the Olympic Games is the ultimate goal of every elite athlete. The selection criteria are very high as the games are only held every four years. Australian athletes may also compete at the Commonwealth Games, which is only open to sportspeople from **Commonwealth** countries.

Grand Prix

To maintain their competitive edge, top athletes participate in Grand Prix events, most of which are held over the Australian spring, summer and early autumn.

Selection Criteria

All championships have selection criteria that must be met by athletes who wish to participate. The selection criteria are set out in a table of qualifying times. For the 2018 Commonwealth Games, the qualifying times for each section were:

MEN A	MEN B	Event	WOMEN A	WOMEN B
10.15	10.24	100m	11.26	11.40
20.44	20.64	200m	23.10	23.40
45.50	46.00	400m	52.10	52.70
01:46:50	01:47:40	800m	02:01:00	02:02:40
03:37:50	03:40:80	1500m	04:08:10	04:10:90
13:22:60	13:35:00	5000m	15:22:00	15:45:50
27:54:00	28:31:20	10000m	32:15:00	33:13:80
02:19:00		Marathon	2:45:00	
08:32:00	08:45:00	3000m SC	09:42:00	09:58:60
13.56	13.71	110m H/100m H	13.01	13.33
49.35	49.98	400m H	56.10	57.30
2.28	2.20	High Jump	1.92	1.85
5.60	5.25	Pole Vault	4.50	4.25
8.09	7.82	Long Jump	6.65	6.39
16.69	16.25	Triple Jump	13.90	13.45
20.00	18.10	Shot Put	17.70	16.42
61.90	59.10	Discus Throw	59.90	54.60
72.10	65.30	Hammer Throw	67.30	61.70
80.80	73.30	Javelin Throw	60.60	54.42
8000	7600	Decathlon/Heptathlon	6000	5600
1:24:00		20km	1:36:00	

World Rankings

All championship-standard athletes in the world are ranked by performance in the IAAF world rankings. The rankings are altered throughout the year, according to performance. To achieve a ranking, athletes must have taken part in a minimum of six IAAF competitions.

Rankings are measured in points. Points are awarded down to eighth place in heats, quarterfinals, semi-finals and finals. Bonus points are awarded for a world record. More points are awarded for some competitions than others. The highest number of points is awarded for Olympics and World Championship results. Other international competitions that score IAAF ranking points are the World Youth Games, World Cup events and the World University Games.

GETTING INVOLVED

Athletics is not only about gold medals and world records. Its most important role in our lives is to help us get fit, stay fit and enjoy the good health that comes with physical fitness. Athletics provides the fun of being involved with teammates and friends on the sporting field. Australian communities are well served by organisations, such as Little Athletics, that help young people become involved in track and field sports. The emphasis is always on participation, not on winning. Through participation, young people gain the opportunity to experience a range of track and field sports, and discover which events they most enjoy.

Numbers

Over 100,000 young people between the ages of five and 15 participate in Little Athletics Australia-wide.

Little Athletics

Athletics has a strong following in Australia at all levels. Children as young as five participate in Little Athletics in every state and territory. The official figures for athletics competitions, from almost 500 centres across Australia, show that over 100,000 young people are participating in athletics every week. Many more Australians over the age of 15 take part in athletics events, including club sports meets, fun runs, mini-marathons and cross-country runs. There are also millions of Australians who belong to jogging clubs and fitness clubs.

What You Can Do

Little Athletics is organised around the skills of running, jumping and throwing. These skills take in all the major track and field sports. Running events include 25, 50, 75, 100, 200, 400 and 800 metres, and include relays. Jumping events include high jump, long jump and triple jump. Throwing events include discus, shot put and javelin. Coaching is provided at every step. Most Little Athletics clubs also organise coaching camps during school holidays, where kids can devote themselves to their favourite sports for a few days at a time – and all the fun activities that go along with participation.

History of Little Athletics

The Little Athletics program began in 1964, when Trevor Billingham, an athletics enthusiast, saw the need for a well-organised Saturday morning get-together of young people who wanted to learn more about track and field sports. He set to work on a sports field in Geelong, encouraging children too young to join in established athletics competition to turn up and have a go. The program grew rapidly, leading to the founding of the Victorian Little Athletics Association in 1967, and to the Australian Little Athletics Union in 1972.

School Visits

Little Athletics centres organise school visits to promote participation. Coaches and well-known athletes show children the fun involved in setting challenges and becoming fitter and stronger.

AUSTRALIA'S OLYMPIC GOLD MEDALLISTS

ATHLETE	YEAR	EVENT
Edwin Flack	Athens, 1896	800 metres and 1500 metres
	Paris, 1900	
	St Louis, 1904	
	London, 1908	
	Stockholm, 1912	
	1916 - suspended during WW I	
Nick Winter	Paris, 1924	Triple jump
	Amsterdam, 1928	
	Los Angeles, 1932	
	Berlin, 1936	
	1940 to 1944 suspended during WWII	
John Winter	London, 1948	High Jump
Marjorie Jackson x 2 Shirley Strickland de la Hunty	Helsinki, 1952	100 metres and 200 metres 80 metres hurdles
Betty Cuthbert x 3 Shirley Strickland de la Hunty x 2 Norma Croker Fleur Mellor	Melbourne, 1956	100 metres, 200 metres and 4 x 100 metres relay 80 metres hurdles and 4 x 100 metres relay 4 x 100 metres relay 4 x 100 metres relay
Herb Elliott	Rome, 1960	1500 metres
Betty Cuthbert	Tokyo, 1964	400 metres
Ralp Doubell Maureen Caird	Mexico City, 1968	80 metres 80 metres hurdles
	Munich, 1972	
	Montreal, 1976	
	Moscow, 1980	
Glynis Nunn	Los Angeles, 1984	Heptathlon
Debbie Flintoff-King	Seoul, 1988	400 metres hurdles
	Barcelona, 1992	
	Atlanta, 1996	
Cathy Freeman	Sydney, 2000	400 metres
	Athens, 2004	
Steven Hooker	Beijing, 2008	Pole Vault
Jared Tallent Sally Pearson	London, 2012	50 kilometre walk 100 metre hurdles
	Rio de Janeiro, 2016	

GLOSSARY

amateur - an athlete who does not receive payment for participating in a sport
Athletics Australia - the national governing body of athletics in Australia
Australian Track and Field Championships - the premier national athletics competition, held in April each year
baton - a metallic tube passed from one runner to another in the course of a relay race
BCE - Before the Common Era
Commonwealth Games - a sporting event held every four years, with participation restricted to members of the Commonwealth of Nations
cross-country - any race run across open land, rather than on an athletics track or road
decathlon - an athletic sporting event comprising 10 separate events
discus - a field event in which athletes attempt to throw a metal disc as far as possible
disqualified - refused permission to take part in or continue in an event, or to have a result not counted, due to a breaking of the rules
elite - the highest level of a sport
Grand Prix - a series of athletics meets restricted to high performing sportspeople
heptathlon - a sporting event comprising seven separate events
high jump - a field event in which athletes attempt to jump over a bar at increasing heights
hurdling - a sporting event held on a running track, in which athletes leap over fences, or hurdles, placed at intervals in their path
javelin - a field event in which athletes attempt to throw a spear-shaped stick as far as possible
International Association of Athletic Federations (IAAF) - the international governing body of athletics
lane - a length-ways division of an athletics track along which an athlete runs during competition
Little Athletics - a national program of coaching and competition in athletics for children
long jump - a field event in which athletes attempt to jump as far as possible onto a bed of sand
marathon - the longest of all Olympic running events, competed over a distance of 41 kilometres
personal best - the best personal result achieved by an athlete in a particular event
pole vault - a field event in which athletes attempt to propel themselves over a bar suspended above the ground using a long, flexible pole
professional - an athlete who accepts payment for training and competing in a sport
relay - a track event where members of a team each take one section of the race
steeplechase - an athletic event held over distances of 3,000 and 6,000 metres in which participants jump over obstacles
stopboard - a curved board at the front of the shot put throwing circle
triple jump - a field event comprising of a hop, a step and a jump
wind assistance - a measurement of the wind speed on the backs of competitors in running events

INDEX